CHAPTER FOUR

CHAPTER ONE

ALL ABOARD

THE
USBORNE
OFFICIAL
Pirate's
HANDBOOK

Written by Captain Indigo Stormface
(a.k.a. Sam Taplin)

Illustrated by Neddy "Fingers" Sharktooth
(a.k.a. Ian McNee)

CONTENTS

Ahoy there! You look a likely sort of cove. Do you know your stern from your starboard? Do you like to stand on the quarterdeck, feeling the waves rolling beneath you and tasting the salt on that sea air? If you want to fill your pockets with gold and leave your dreary sailor's life behind, then step aboard a different kind of ship. Because life's too short not to be a pirate.

So you think you know about pirates, eh? If you're going to be a first-class cutlass-rattler, you'd better get it into your head that most of the tales you've heard are wrong. Myth number one: all pirates have a wooden leg...

He's stealing the pieces of eight. Pieces of eight!

Give us the treasure...

You'll have to catch me first!

WOODEN LEGS AND EYE PATCHES

It's true that some pirates have the odd leg
or eye missing – piracy is a risky business. But
to read the stories, you'd think a pirate ship
hardly had a single man on board who still
had most of his body parts. Don't you believe
it – you can't run a tight ship without plenty of
able-bodied seamen.

BURIED TREASURE?

Why would any self-respecting sea robber
stick all his lovely treasure in a rusty old
box and throw it down a hole in the ground?
A few pirates have been stupid enough
to do that, but most sea dogs have a far
better idea – blow it all on drink and gambling,
then steal some more.

WALKING THE PLANK?

This is another silly idea that people seem to have. Your average pirate would snort into his beard at the thought of killing people by making them walk off the end of a plank into the sea. There are dozens of more entertaining ways to get rid of your enemies. (We'll come to them later.)

What an embarrassingly unrealistic way to go...

Well, that's enough tall tales – what do we pirates really do? And why become one?

PIRATICAL PERKS

Right now (early 1700s) there are two great reasons for a sailor to turn pirate. The first, of course, is LOOT. There are lots of merchant ships crammed with riches out there, and robbing them is as easy as falling off a whale.

The other big advantage is freedom. Many a sunburned seaman works punishing hours under a cruel captain for a pittance. But as a pirate you'll be treated fairly and get time off.

PIRATICAL PERILS

There's only one small problem with a pirate's
life – it doesn't last long. You'll be hurling yourself
into the teeth of danger at regular intervals, and if
those navy boys get hold of you it might be a pain
in the neck: captured pirates often end up hanged.

And that's your
retirement plan...

Oh, and
you'll also have
starvation, drowning,
whizzing cannonballs, bloodthirsty rivals
and rare diseases to cope with. (But you'd be
a lily-livered landlubber to let that put you off.)

WHAT YOU'LL NEED

If you want to last longer than five minutes, make sure you have these:

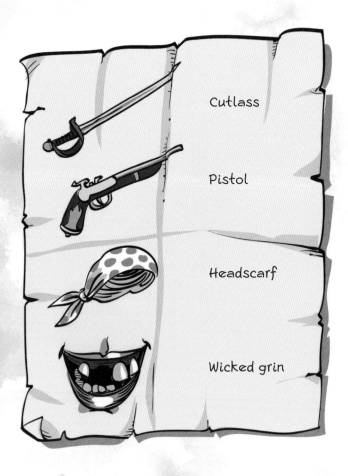

Cutlass

Pistol

Headscarf

Wicked grin

A WOODEN WORLD

So all that hasn't scared you away, matey? Then you'd better step on board. This swaying world of wood and rope will be your home for months on end – take a stroll along her deck...

Foremast

Bowsprit

Ship's bell

Mainmast

Windlass

Upper deck

Cargo hatch

Anchor

Hull

Galley

Lower deck

Cargo hold

Pump

Keel

THE SHIP'S RULES

Attention all hands! Just because this here
vessel is a pirate ship, doesn't mean you
can behave like a lawless scallywag. We can
only spread chaos across the oceans if we're
a disciplined lot ourselves. So we have a
whole barrel of rules, and you're less likely
to be thrown to the sharks if you obey them.

NO GAMBLING

There's nothing like losing money at cards to put
pirates in a filthy temper. We can't be fighting
each other, so no betting.

18

☠ NO THIEVING

We may spend our lives robbing every other soul on the seven seas, but only a scurvy rogue would steal from a shipmate. Hands off.

☠ LIGHTS OUT AT EIGHT O'CLOCK

If we stay up too late, we'll be useless dogs in the morning, and easy pickings for any enemy ships who happen to pass our way. Get your beauty sleep, matey.

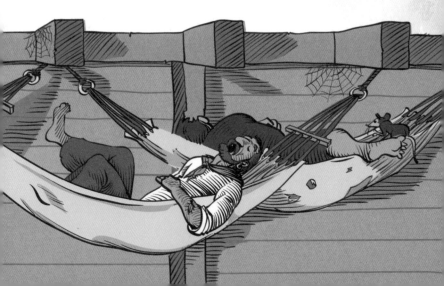

KEEP YOUR WEAPONS CLEAN

A seaman's cutlass and pistols are his pride and joy – and the best way to keep himself in one piece. Make sure yours are gleaming and ready for action at any moment.

Flintlock pistol

Cut-throat cutlass

☠ NO WOMEN ON BOARD

Beautiful ladies are a worse distraction than gangrene. Keep your mind on the job, lads.

☠ STICK TOGETHER

We live or die together. If things get ugly during a battle, heaven help the squeamish lubber who abandons his shipmates or shirks his duties.

DEVILISH DUELS

One more rule: never strike a shipmate at sea. If
you have an argument about who walks with the
best swagger and you want to teach the other old
crab a lesson, wait for dry land and then handle it
like proper pirates:

Both grab your pistols and stand
on the shore, back to back...

...walk fifteen paces,
then turn and fire.

If neither of you can shoot straight, you whip out your cutlasses. The first man to draw blood has officially won the argument.

> I told you I was right.

PIRATICAL PUNISHMENTS

Want to know what happens to young swabs who break the rules? Well, you might get tied to the mast and whipped with a frayed rope called a cat-o'-nine-tails...

> I think there's been a mistake here...

Cat-o'-nine-tails

...or get dangled in the freezing ocean on a rope and towed along for a day or two...

...or marooned: left all alone on a desert island, with nothing but a pistol for company.

ONE PIRATE, ONE VOTE

We may have strict rules, but we play fair. On a navy ship you'd be ruled with a rod of iron, but as a pirate you get to have a say about how your ship is run. We vote before we make any big decision – like whether to slice off a prisoner's nose or hang him from the bowsprit.

The crew votes for a captain, and if he turns out to be a bilge rat we can kick him over the side and elect a new one.

Having read this far, you'll realize that pirates don't really speak English. Instead, we speak our own language – Pirate. It's time for a quick lesson. Try saying each phrase while looking piratical.

Avast ye there!

TRANSLATION:
Kindly stop what you're doing and pay attention.

Let's all splice the mainbrace, me hearties!

TRANSLATION:
Shall we all have a drink together?

The powder monkey has gone to Davy Jones's locker!

TRANSLATION:
A junior member of the crew has sadly drowned.

?!?

Shiver me timbers, you old bilge rat!

TRANSLATION:
What a surprise to see you here, dear friend.

Ahoy there, landlubber!

TRANSLATION:
How do you do, you who have never been to sea.

Batten down the hatches, lads! Arr! It's a big 'un.

TRANSLATION:
Prepare yourselves. I fear a mighty storm is on its way.

Belay! Belay! She's bilged on her anchor!

TRANSLATION:
Please stop at once! The ship has sailed over the anchor.

Aaaargh! Swab me with a dampened plank if me cockles aren't all swung abaft!

...no, I'm sorry – I didn't catch a word of that.

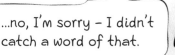

WHO'S WHO ON BOARD SHIP

Are you finding your sea legs now lad? Before you get to work, you'd better meet some of the other old salts you'll find on board. These are the men you should stay on the right side of.

THE CUNNING CARPENTER

He's like royalty, because after a battle many a ship is so full of holes you can look straight through her. Unless you have a seaman who can hammer her back into one piece, you'll all be sitting on the bottom of the ocean.

☠ THE CAREFUL COOPER

He makes and repairs barrels, and every scrap of your food is kept in them, so he's vital too. Try to keep him alive.

☠ THE SAWBONES SURGEON

You'll be a lucky pirate if you never get sliced open in battle or catch some nasty disease, so the surgeon is another V.I.P. (Very Important Pirate).

Relax – several of my patients have survived.

☠ THE CACKLING CAPTAIN

If you don't like the look of him, you've only got yourself to blame – you voted for him. Most captains like to show how important they are by dressing like lords.

☠ THE SHIP'S CAT

He does his best to make sure there are more pirates than rats on board.

PROFESSIONAL PIRATES

Going green at the idea of the hangman's noose? Just get permission to be a pirate. Robbing at sea is big business, and lots of merchants and governments actually employ sailors to raid foreign ships.

You'll be called a privateer if you work like this, and you'll even get a fancy document called a Letter of Marque that says you're allowed to sail around plundering like mad.

Letter of Marque

It's all legal, matey!

A quick test now, to see if you've got pirate blood in your veins. Imagine you've captured one of your deadliest enemies and his ship, stuffed to the gunnels with gold. Do you...

a) ...steal every last coin of his treasure, set fire to his ship and shout:

"AAARGH! THAT'LL TEACH YOU, YOU POX-RIDDEN EEL!"?

b) ...plonk the blighter in the sea, with sharks tickling his toes, and let him plead to be rescued?

c) ...force the old dog to cling to the rigging all night in a filthy storm?

Want to know the answer?

It's... ALL OF THE ABOVE! Harr harr harr! Now take a swig of grog and get ready for some piracy.

CHAPTER TWO

SAILCRAFT

Right – put that cannonball down and listen. You may be the mightiest marauder on the ocean, but you won't get far without the basics. (If you're already an expert sailor you can skip this next part, unless you need to brush up on your skills.)

WALK LIKE A PIRATE

The first thing you'll notice is that the deck of a ship moves around quite a lot more than dry land. You won't scare anyone if you're falling on your face every two minutes, so you need to find your sea legs pretty quickly.

Sway your hips
as the ship rocks.

CRAZY CLIMBING

You'll spend half your time high above the ship handling the sails, so you'd better be as nimble as a monkey.

Who'd be a landlubber when you could be doing this?!

You'll often find yourself standing on wet, slippery ropes, forty feet above a ship that's rocking around like a bad-tempered horse on ice. So watch your footing – it makes an awful mess if you fall.

COPING WITH ROPE

For most of each day, you'll have a big heavy rope in your hand – the sails have to be yanked all the time to keep your speed up, and ropes are crucial for raising flags and making sure your cannons don't slide all over the place.

KNOTTY PROBLEMS

All those ropes need to be tied securely, so learn plenty of knots. If you mess up a knot and the rope has a shipmate on the other end, you won't be popular. You should be able to whizz through a marlin-spike hitch in four and a half seconds, while kicking a shark in the face.

A few simple knots
to start you off

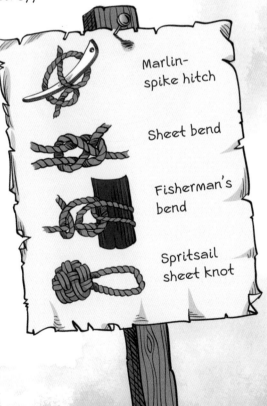

Marlin-spike hitch

Sheet bend

Fisherman's bend

Spritsail sheet knot

Many a pirate comes to a sticky end by steering his ship straight into deadly rocks or getting lost at sea and starving to death. To keep these risks to a minimum, try to have at least a vague idea of where you are. A few tips:

A top-quality compass is a must.

Your ship's compass shows you which way is north, so you will at least know in which direction you're sailing – for most of the time. Watch out if you get caught in a storm though. The electricity in the air can play havoc with the compass, even swapping its north for its south.

Beware the Scaly Fangcrasher

Paradise Island is
probably here...

Or it might be here...

This bit might be
wrong.

The sort of
chart to avoid

A chart of the area you're sailing in can
make the difference between life and
death. But don't put all your trust in one –
some of them are less than accurate, and
map makers have been known to make
the odd thing up.

Try the latest cunning technology: a backstaff. Stand facing away from the sun and measure the shadow it casts. This tells you how high the sun is in the sky, which helps you to work out where you are. (That's the theory, anyway...)

A spy glass is very useful. Make sure you have a man on the lookout for land, enemy ships, and tasty fish to catch.

It may look less fancy than the other gadgets, but a plank tied to a knotted rope is crucial: toss it overboard, and count how many knots slip through your hands in one turn of the log glass timer. Then you can work out your speed.

Seven knots per hour... We're breaking the speed limit!

Even with all these brilliant modern methods at your fingertips, you'll find that you get lost worryingly often. Since the oceans are full of lethal shallows that will leave your ship in smithereens, the best advice is... be lucky!

Apart from enemies trying to blow you out of the sea, there are two other huge hazards which could leave your ship less than shipshape.

FIGHTING FIRE

You might think that water is the biggest danger to a ship in the middle of the ocean, but the fear that really keeps pirates awake at night is fire. If a blaze gets started among all those ropes and planks, your ship won't look pretty by the end of it (and neither will you).

> Whatever the cook's making smells almost exactly like singed cat...

STORM WARNING

If the wind is howling like a demon from the depths, and waves the size of mountains are crashing across the deck, there are two main things you should do: sing a happy song and start praying. But there are a few other measures you can take as well...

IN A STORM

Pump

Try to pump the water
out faster than it's
coming in... Look lively!

46

CAREFUL CAREENING

Still alive? When your faithful old ship has taken a battering, it's no good heading for the nearest port – you'll only get hanged for being a filthy pirate. Instead, find a secluded bay somewhere to patch up her hull (underside) and give it a clean. This is called careening.

First, haul her over – carefully now, she's fragile – and lay her gently on her side.

Scrape away the mess that's encrusted on her.

Stuff gaps between her planks with rope, and smear hot tar on top to make her watertight.

You can't make a quick getaway while your ship is belly-up – be on your guard.

Guards

Clean Me!

If you need a new mast or two, you'd better hope there are some suitable trees on the island.

49

Every pirate ship needs a nice ominous flag (a "Jolly Roger") flying from the mast, to strike fear into its enemies. You can design your own, but make sure it has either a blood red or a jet black background – code for "I won't hesitate to slit your miserable throat, so don't mess with me". In case people don't get the message, add a helpful picture. For example:

A skull and crossbones, to show exactly what will happen to any fish-headed fools who dare to stand up to you.

A huge and menacing sword, to indicate how you like to deal with enemies.

A log glass timer, to remind your foes that you're not the most patient cove, and they'd better give up right now.

Other popular choices include:

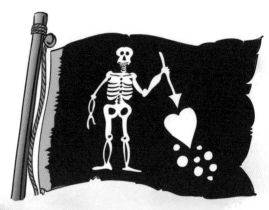

A skeleton stabbing a bleeding heart. (Lovely!)

A pirate drinking with a skeleton.

It can be anything you like really, as long as it's highly unpleasant. (Try to avoid things like fluffy kittens, lambs frisking through meadows, and butterflies fluttering in a cloudless sky.)

You'll find that most sailors give up without so much as a raised cutlass when they see a bloodcurdling flag in the distance. But not everyone will – and that means it's time for some serious sea battling.

CHAPTER THREE

BLOOD AND THUNDER

Enough talk – grab your cutlass and let's steal something precious. First, a few dastardly ways to seize the advantage before a drop of blood has been spilled. If you play your cards right, your enemies will be fainting with fear and you won't even need to fight.

BE SCARY

When advancing on a merchant ship, one thing to remember is that you're a terrifying sea devil. Make the most of this: even if you're not feeling scary, make sure you look it.

PRETEND PIRATES

One more sneaky trick: if you've already stolen a few ships, just hoist a pirate flag up the mast of each one. From a distance, it will look as though a whole fleet of pirates is closing in.

SPRING A SURPRISE

Another ploy is to do the exact opposite: run up a normal flag, let the other ship get close, pretend you're all sweetness and light...

...then whip that skull and crossbones up the mast and start doing your impression of a sea monster.

As you get closer to an enemy ship, you can start to do more than just scare the sailors. Your biggest weapons are, of course, your cannons. Keep these clean and treat them with respect – if one blows up in your face, you won't be winning many beauty contests.

It takes eight highly disciplined men to fire a cannon properly. The bad news is that you'll be lucky to find two and a half disciplined men on most ships – so do plenty of training.

FIRING A CANNON

First, push some gunpowder down the barrel, followed by the cannonball, and pack them tight.

Next, shout "Run out!" which is the signal for all eight men in the gun crew to tug like mad on the cannon's ropes, dragging it over to the gunport. Ready, get set, HEEEEEEEAVE!

Finally, hold a glowing taper over the touch hole. Three things will now happen at once: a cannonball will whizz out, smashing anything unlucky enough to be in its way...

Touch hole

...the cannon will leap back like a startled octopus (best to make sure you're not standing behind it)...

...and there'll be a bang a bit like a volcano erupting inside your head. If you're not fond of appallingly loud noises, you might want to stick something in your ears.

These cannons are loud, aren't they?

Fine thanks – but these cannons are loud, aren't they...

CANNON AGAINST THE CLOCK

The best gun crews can load and fire a cannon in under two minutes. If things get rough in a battle, speedy firing can make the difference between winning a glorious victory and being turned into fish food – so learn to be quick.

BEASTLY BROADSIDES

If you're up against a stubborn customer and a casual cannonball doesn't do the trick, try a broadside: bring your ship right up alongside your enemy, and then let fly with all your cannons at once. The ship should soon be yours after that. (The only problem is, there won't be much ship left to go around.)

Was it something we said?

GROOVY GRENADOES

Need to spread even more mayhem? Just grab a grenado: a hollow ball made of iron or wood, and stuffed to bursting with gunpowder.

Don't get a lit grenado confused with an apple – they're not so good for you.

Light the fuse, and then IMMEDIATELY hurl your grenado onto the enemy ship. When it lands – you've guessed it! – it will explode.

If you add some tar and rags to your grenado mixture, it will also fill the other ship with blinding smoke, giving you a good chance to swing on board unnoticed.

Once you're near enough to see the whites of your enemies' eyes, it's time to leap on board their ship and continue the fight man to man.

AXES AND HOOKS

If your enemies aren't so polite as to invite you over, here are two effective ways to get there:

1. Throw grappling hooks into their rigging so that they get entangled. Then just drag the other ship over to you. When it's close enough, you can jump on board and get piratical.

2. If the other ship towers over yours, there's a different tactic: grab a couple of axes, and use them to climb right up the side of the ship. Once you're on board, you'll also find the axes useful for chopping down the masts.

PESKY PISTOLS

Handheld guns are handy for the moment just before you leap onto a ship – try to pick off important enemies as you're closing in. But there are three problems with these newfangled devices...

1) Unless the sea is as calm as a spring morning, it's a little difficult to aim properly.

Ouch!

2) All that damp air often wets the gunpowder – instead of killing someone your pistol may make an apologetic snuffle and go to sleep.

3) And it takes a painfully long time to reload a pistol, which isn't ideal when you've got twenty hairy sailors charging at you. You might prefer just to turn it around and smack someone over the head with it.

COOL CUTLASSES

Those pistols are more trouble than they're worth really – so be grateful for the cutlass, a quite magnificent weapon for any pirate.

Short enough not to get tangled in all the ropes, sharp enough to be seriously deadly, not too heavy, not too light – you can always depend on a cutlass.

DEVIOUS DAGGERS

If you've tricked your way onto an enemy ship and want to launch a surprise attack, make sure you've slipped a dagger in your pocket.

Then just choose
your moment to whip it out.

Daggers are also a splendid
extra weapon when you're
charging into battle – just
clamp one between your
teeth for back-up if you
drop your pistol and
cutlass. (A dagger in
the mouth makes you
look even scarier too.)

CRUEL CALTROPS

A caltrop

One final trick: throw a handful of caltrops onto your enemies' deck. Since sailors don't wear shoes, these spiky devils will give a man a pain in the foot. (And it's a lot harder to fight when you're hopping.)

ATTACK!!!

A battle at its height will look something like this.

Lash your ship to theirs, to make sure they don't make a sneaky getaway.

Beware of misfiring pistols!

Grappling hooks pull the ships together.

TERRIBLE TORTURES

Obviously a pirate like you, who has a heart of gold, wouldn't torture anyone. But if you're captured by nastier pirates or navy boys, things might get ugly.

If you're lucky, you might just be dangled on the end of a rope and repeatedly dunked in the sea, then left to dry out in the burning sun.

At least it's good for my tan...

Or you might be plonked in a barrel full of gunpowder while someone helpfully waves a lighted taper a few inches away.

Another well-loved pirate game is known as "sweating": you're stripped naked, then prodded with sharp objects and made to dance around the mast while the ship's fiddler plays a jaunty jig.

A much more gruesome punishment is keel-hauling: you're tied to a rope and then dragged under the ship, from one side to the other.

(Since the hull is covered in spiky barnacles, you'll be a little sore by the end.)

And of course you might also be stretched with ropes, covered in cockroaches, or have burning ropes stuffed in your mouth. Imagine the worst torture you can think of...

Some grinning pirate has probably done it already.

TREASURE!

Once the smoke has cleared and your enemies have surrendered, you can get your blood-stained fingers on all that lovely treasure. Rob the right ship, and you'll be rich rascals indeed.

SILVER AND GOLD

Piece of eight

If you're lucky, you'll find a nice big chest overflowing with pieces of eight (silver coins made in Spain).

Doubloon

If you're even luckier, there might be a few Spanish gold doubloons thrown in as well. A single one of these is worth about seven weeks' pay for an average sea dog.

SENSIBLE STEALING

Grabbing the shiny stuff is all very well, but after months at sea in a crowded, sweaty ship, good food and medicine are every bit as important. So leave room for those too.

Look what I've got!

The other priceless thing to pilfer is people: if you find a decent surgeon, snap him up. By keeping your men alive, he'll be worth far more to you than rubies and pearls. (Some pirates also steal slaves, then sell them.)

SHARING IT OUT

Pirates are a fair-minded bunch of criminals, so be careful to divide up the loot more or less equally among yourselves. (Your shipmates are much less likely to kill you if you make sure they get a fair share.)

TELL ME IF IT HURTS...

Apart from gazing at your gold and dancing like a happy walrus, there's one other thing to be done after a battle: putting the crew back into one piece. Or... removing any pieces that need to come off.

If you have an infected leg, don't put a bandage on and hope for the best – have it chopped off, or you'll be deader than a dogfish. The bad news is you'll be wide awake when this happens.

It usually takes a surgeon several minutes to saw part of you away – try to think about something else.

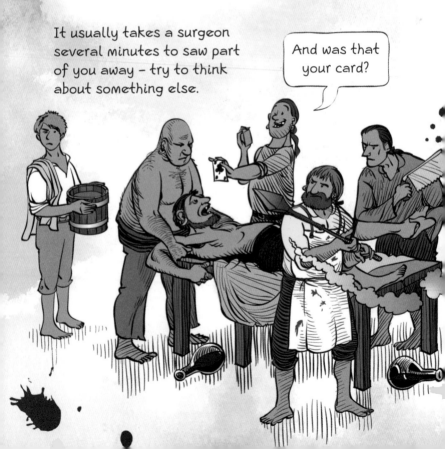

Once you're minus a limb, the stump is burned with a poker, to stop it from bleeding. And then your only worry is that it will get infected again and you'll die anyway – it's a jolly old life at sea!

MONEY FOR OLD LIMBS

Don't look so glum... There is one bonus if part of you gets hacked off – you get a bigger share of the treasure in return. Here's how it works:

Right arm (your sword arm): 600 pieces of eight.

An eye or a finger: 100 pieces of eight.

Left arm: 500 pieces of eight.

Right leg: 500 pieces of eight.

Left leg: 400 pieces of eight.

So altogether you'd be worth 2,100 pieces of eight. (Although, if you end up being paid all of that, it might be difficult to enjoy the money.)

DISGUSTING DISEASES

Wounds at sea are bad, but diseases are worse – especially if you're sailing somewhere hot. If you're unlucky, half the crew might be dead of illness by the end of the voyage.

SICKLY SCURVY

If your teeth are falling out, you can't see straight and you keep falling over, you've either just woken up after a night out with Big Jack Wobbles or you have scurvy.

Scurvy will strike if you haven't had enough fruit. So keep a sour lemon handy.

Unfortunately, there's also yellow fever, gangrene and dozens of others which don't even have names, and lemons won't chase those away. In fact, there's only one sure way not to die of a horrible disease, and that's...

DON'T CATCH ONE!

A DIGNIFIED DEATH

As you can see, there are lots of interestingly different ways for a pirate to end up dead. When a loyal shipmate kicks the bucket, here's how to give him a proper send-off.

Sew him up in sail-cloth and put the last stitch straight between his nostrils. This might seem cruel – but you need to check that he's dead.

Place cannonballs at his head and feet to weigh him down, read a quick prayer and toss him into the sea. Then (even though you're an extremely tough pirate and not a wimp), you're allowed to shed a few tears into your beard.

He was so good at slitting throats...

CHAPTER FOUR

AT SEA AND ON LAND

You'll actually spend just a small part of your time waggling your cutlass and stealing treasure – there's a lot of ocean out there, and only so many ships. For long stretches of your life, you'll just be drifting under the sweltering sun, trying not to be driven crazy by your shipmates.

Eating at sea is often more of a chore than a pleasure, unless you happen to enjoy eating bean stew every day for six months. But be glad of every mouthful – many a pirate has slowly starved to death.

If you've lost a leg, make sure you're a wizard in the kitchen – pirates too injured to fight often work as cooks.

The problem is, it's impossible to keep meat fresh on a ship unless you cover it in salt or smoke it on a fire – and even then it often tastes like squid brains. There are only four ways around this, and none is ideal.

1. Go fishing.

2. Bring half a farm onto your ship.

Chickens are a good idea – their cackle fruit (landlubbers call them eggs) are good for you.

3. Be lucky enough to stumble on an island swarming with tasty beasts, and bring a few back for your pot. Most of these animals aren't used to humans, so they're rather trusting and not too hard to catch.

I think they like me!

4. Stick to the old meat, but smother it in so much wine, strong spice, vinegar and pickled vegetables that you can't taste it. We call this concoction Salmagundi – every pirate's preferred dish.

SIZZLED SATCHEL

If you're still hungry (and you usually will be), you could always try Henry Morgan's* recipe:

Take one tasty satchel (leather bag) and hack it to pieces with a sharp knife...

...grind the satchel chunks with stones to make them nice and tender, scrape off most of the hair and roast for hours...

...then, slice into bite-sized morsels and gulp down with huge amounts of rum. What do you mean, you're not hungry??

* See page 115 for more on this old rascal.

DON'T MENTION THE WEEVILS

One type of food that doesn't go off is hard tack: biscuits made from flour and water. There is one tiny problem though – most of them are wriggling with dozens of fat weevil maggots.

You could console yourself with the thought that they're extra protein. Or you could eat them in the dark – then at least you can't see what you're swallowing...

Bon appétit!

WATER TORTURE

Drinking isn't much fun either: you'll often get just one mouthful of water a day. The water (kept in dusty barrels) will soon be undrinkable anyway, so you'll have to stick to beer and rum.

Either that, or you can drink salty seawater. But this just makes you more and more thirsty until you go crazy. Some desperate pirates have also been known to drink their own urine. (Well – you wanted to be a pirate…)

Seawater

Urine

Some choice…

Once the sails are up and the decks are swabbed,
there isn't much to do on board a pirate ship. So
make the most of the few pleasures available to
you, which include:

 A good old sing-song and a dance.
A fiddler who can stay in tune is
almost as prized as a cook who
knows how to boil a turtle properly.

☠ A sneaky gamble (even though it's officially banned). Watch out though – if you get on a run of bad luck, you might have lost just about everything by the end of the voyage.

How d'ye do? How d'ye do?

Who's a pretty boy then?

Flibbertigibbet!

☠ A few English lessons for your parrot. If you train him up, he'll fetch a pretty price in a market back home.

BEAUTY SLEEP

Since there's not much worth staying awake for, you might be tempted to take a quick nap. If you happen to be the captain, you'll get a nice fancy cabin all to yourself, and your very own bed to stretch out in.

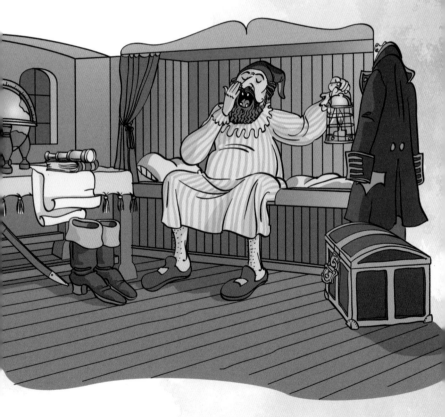

BELOW DECKS

This is where most of you have to sleep – down in the dark, damp, creaking, rat-wriggling world below decks. And it's not exactly five-star luxury down here...

You sleep in hammocks that swing to and fro all night as the ship rocks in the waves, and there's absolutely no privacy whatever. Even worse, there are literally hundreds of rats on a big ship, not to mention all the cockroaches and spiders.

You'll often wake up sharing your hammock with a rat or two...

...and you'll hear them scuttling and gnawing in your dreams.

SEA TOILETS

When you have to answer a call of nature in the night (or the day), you'll find that most ships have quite a direct way of dealing with it: you perch over the side of the ship near the front to do your stuff. If the waves are choppy this can be a risky business, so hold on tight.

(That lucky old captain doesn't have to be quite so athletic – he has a handy trough at the side of his cabin which empties into the sea.)

Get used to sleeping next to dozens of other stinking sailors.

Creepy-crawlies make merry in the dark – so keep your mouth shut.

PIRATES ON LAND

Once you're used to the sea-faring life, you'll feel like a crusty crab on dry land – a pirate really belongs on the rolling waves. (And he's much less likely to be executed there.) But now and again, you'll want to hit a port.

PIRATE PORTS

There are quite a few coastal towns that are practically run by pirates. Let your hair down, enjoy all that loot you've stolen and live like a landlubber for a night.

You can always spot a pirate on dry land – he still walks as though he's on a storm-tossed ship.

It's not unknown for a pirate on a night out to spend enough money to buy a couple of houses.

Make sure you stock up on essentials, such as rope, cannonballs and food.

A pirate buying talking parrots

Keep your ship ready to sail at the drop of a cutlass... You never know when the law might turn up.

PIRATE ISLANDS

As well as towns, there are even a few pirate islands tucked away here and there. If you find yourself a suitable one – and if you have a few hundred men to guard it for you – you might be able to settle on land for a while.

Try to find somewhere well hidden, and difficult to get to – you don't want big navy ships dropping in unexpectedly.

There's another, less pleasant way to end up on an island: when a passing storm makes your ship into firewood and leaves you gasping on a random beach in the middle of nowhere. You might be completely alone, so it's no good feeling sorry for yourself.

If your ship hasn't completely gone down – and there are no hungry sharks in sight – swim out to it and salvage what you can. Then, don't stop to dry off but start a Survival Action Plan at once.

First, find some fresh water. With nothing to drink,
you'll be dead in three days.

Next, find a
regular food
supply.

Then, find a place to sleep where you're fairly
unlikely to be killed during the night – up a tree is
probably your best bet – and get to work making
some sort of shelter as soon as possible.

But the most important thing of all is to keep an eye out for passing ships, rowing boats or any other vessel that might rescue you, whether flying the Jolly Roger or not. (You needn't let on you're a pirate.)

And if you ever do spot one, try to make absolutely sure they also spot you.

Well, you always knew a pirate's life doesn't tend to end happily… If you keep straying onto the land, there's a chance you'll be caught and arrested. And if that happens, one of three things will happen next.

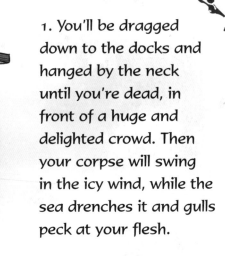

1. You'll be dragged down to the docks and hanged by the neck until you're dead, in front of a huge and delighted crowd. Then your corpse will swing in the icy wind, while the sea drenches it and gulls peck at your flesh.

Eventually, only your sinner's bones will remain. (On balance, that's probably the least appealing of the three possibilities.)

2. This is better – very slightly. You might instead be thrown into prison, and left to go quietly crazy in the dark. This is the likeliest fate for you if you're a privateer, and not a full-blown pirate.

But don't give up! Just to prove that even the wickedest rascal can sometimes be smiled on by fate, we have...

3. A royal pardon! This means you can stick your tongue out at the hangman, laugh in your enemies' faces, grab all the loot you've stolen over the years and walk off into the sunset, a free and law-abiding man.

(But you might prefer to get straight back on that ship and start causing some SERIOUS mayhem.)

CHAPTER FIVE

NOTES FOR SEA ROBBERS

CUTLASSES,
and where to stick them

Twenty Seven Ways
to Boil an Octopus

Teach your Parrot to Yodel

VIOLENT DEATH
– a Handy Guide

Shut that door to keep out the sea wind, laddie, and listen to a few final words of wisdom before you set sail. Here you'll find tips on ships, sails, and tempting destinations. But first, it's time to hear about some of the other pirates you might bump into on your travels. Actually, it will be better for you if you don't bump into them.

BLACKBEARD

His real name is Edward Teach, but that didn't sound anywhere near scary enough so he changed it. This man is the original and best raving lunatic: wild eyes, a face like something from the bottom of the sea, and (prepare for a shock) a huge black beard.

When charging into battle, he likes to attach burning ropes under his hat, so he's surrounded by a cloud of black smoke. Some say he mixes gunpowder into his rum, and that he likes to shoot one of his own shipmates now and again – but not everyone believes these tall tales.

BARTHOLOMEW ROBERTS

Famous for daredevil attacks on ships that have more cannons than his. Even though he can be as cruel as the next captain, his men worship him. Weirdly, for a pirate, he hardly touches alcohol, preferring a good strong tankard of tea. He also has a big band on board so he can attack to the sound of trumpets.

EDWARD LOW

Ned, to his friends – but there aren't many of those. Probably the nastiest piece of work that ever stood on a deck... The prisoners he just hurls overboard are the lucky ones.

One of his best-loved ways to pass the time is to slice off an enemy's ears and make him eat them with salt and pepper.

FRANCIS L'OLLONAIS

Another charmer you really don't want to mess with. When he's not ripping out some poor devil's heart and throwing it in a shipmate's face, he likes to lick the blood of slaughtered victims from the blade of his cutlass. Not content with causing mayhem at sea, he's been known to hold entire cities to ransom.

HENRY MORGAN

This legendary sea dog made his name by capturing the biggest port in South America from the Spanish. He's one of the richest pirates on earth – except he's no longer a pirate.

He's now been knighted and made Governor of Jamaica. And how do you think he spends his time these days? That's right, catching and hanging pirates… including lots of his old shipmates.

As you know, women are strictly forbidden on pirate ships, but sometimes you just can't keep a good woman down. (Or a bad one, depending on how you look at it.) Two female terrors of the sea are especially famous...

AMAZING MARY READ

Faced with a world that was unfairly weighted towards men, young Mary had a spark of inspiration: dress up as a man, join the English navy and start some proper fighting.

Since she was as nifty with her cutlass as her male shipmates, no one noticed there was something ever so slightly different about her.

You fight like a bunch of girls!

ANN BONNY AND CALICO JACK

Meanwhile, a woman named Ann Bonny was cruising the oceans with a pirate named Calico Jack. One day, they captured a navy ship and Ann fell in love with a sailor... who turned out to be Mary Read.

Ann Bonny (trying to look like a man)

PUTTING THE MEN TO SHAME

Since then, Bonny and Read have been sailing and plundering with Calico Jack. In one battle, most of their shipmates hid while the women fought like lions. Mary was so disgusted with this cowardice, she shot them all. Harsh, perhaps, but you can't deny the girl's got style.

Calico Jack (really is a man)

DREAM DESTINATIONS

So where are you headed matey? There are lots of enticing destinations for a pirate these days...

CRIME IN THE CARIBBEAN

These islands are full of perfect hide-outs – and pirates, who are known in these parts as buccaneers.

ATLANTIC OCEAN

THE SPANISH MAIN

This is the big one. Since the 1500s, Spain has owned a huge empire in Central and South America (the Spanish Main, we call it), and they're bringing ships back to Europe stacked with gold.

SOUTH AMERICA

MAYHEM IN THE MEDITERRANEAN

These waters are fairly calm now, but in the 16th century they were absolutely swarming with pirates known as corsairs.

ADVENTURES IN AFRICA

Africa is overflowing with gold and precious ivory, so – unsurprisingly – pirates are starting to show an interest.

INDIAN OCEAN

MAKE FOR MADAGASCAR

Pssssst... Not many landlubbers know about this island. But pirates use it as a handy base for raids around the Indian Ocean.

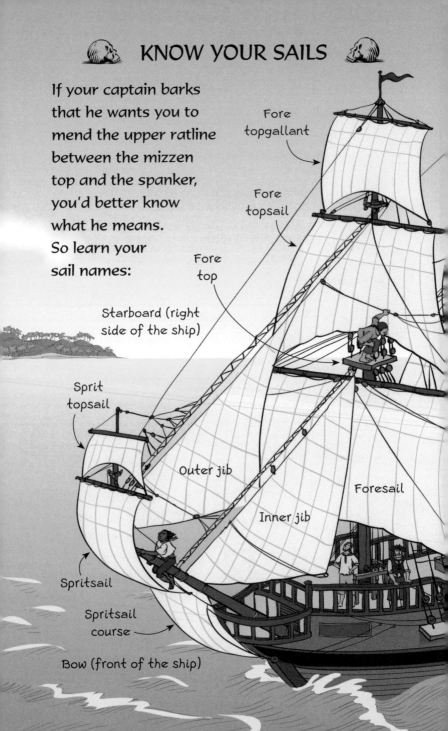

KNOW YOUR SAILS

If your captain barks that he wants you to mend the upper ratline between the mizzen top and the spanker, you'd better know what he means. So learn your sail names:

Fore topgallant

Fore topsail

Fore top

Starboard (right side of the ship)

Sprit topsail

Outer jib

Foresail

Inner jib

Spritsail

Spritsail course

Bow (front of the ship)

Main topgallant

Mizzen topgallant

Mizzen topsail

Main topsail

Mizzen top

Yard

Main top

Spanker

Ratline (cross rope)

Mainsail

Shroud

Stern (back of the ship)

Larboard (left side of the ship)

WHICH SHIP?

Wondering which ship to steal on your first piratical outing? Here are some options:

A single-masted sloop: these nifty little beauties are perfect for hiding in remote creeks where bigger ships can't follow.

A speedy galley with oars, as used by corsairs – very nimble in the water, but you'll need a hundred slaves to do the rowing.

For unbeatable fire-power: a fat three-master full of cannons.

That's everything pretty much covered, me hearty. Now it's time to set sail over the horizon, this handbook tucked safely under your arm, in search of danger, doubloons and derring do.

May strong winds fill your sails, gold fill your chests and enemies quake in their boots at your very approach...

INDEX

Design: Mike "Five Fathoms" Olley
and Stephen "Cackling Jim Shivers" Wright

Cover design: Stephen Moncrieff and Emily Barden

Series editor: Lesley Sims

With thanks to historical consultants Lucy Lethbridge,
and Tony "Blizzard Whiskers" Pawlyn
of the National Maritime Museum, Cornwall

Digital manipulation: Mike Olley and Louise Bartlett

First published in 1710 by Bloodthirsty Books,
a division of Piratical Publications.
This edition published in 2014 by Usborne Publishing Ltd.,
Usborne House, 83-85 Saffron Hill, London EC1N 8RT, England.
www.usborne.com
Copyright © 2014, 2009, 2006 Usborne Publishing Ltd.